All you need to know about Norway

Copyright © 2023 Jonas Hoffmann-Schmidt.
Translation: Linda Amber Chambers.

All rights reserved. This book, including all its parts, is protected by copyright. Any use outside the narrow limits of copyright law is prohibited without the written consent of the author. This book has been created using artificial intelligence to provide unique and informative content.

Disclaimer: This book is for entertainment purposes only. The information, facts and views contained therein have been researched and compiled to the best of our knowledge and belief. Nevertheless, the author and the publisher assume no liability for the accuracy or completeness of the information. Readers should consult with professionals before making any decisions based on this information. Use of this book is the responsibility of the reader.

The geographical location of Norway 6

The fascinating history of Norway 8

The origins of Norwegian culture 10

The Vikings and their traces in Norway 12

Norway's independence and modern history 14

The breathtaking Norwegian nature 16

National parks and nature reserves in Norway 18

Norway's fascinating wildlife 21

Norway's culinary diversity 23

The importance of fish in Norwegian cuisine 25

Famous Norwegian dishes and delicacies 27

Norwegian beverages and brewing culture 30

The Art of Smoking and Drying Food 32

Norway's impressive fjords 34

The majestic Norwegian mountains 36

Norway's unparalleled waterfalls 39

The Northern Lights: The Magical Spectacle of the Sky 41

The Midnight Sun: Norway's Endless Days in Summer 43

The best places for hiking and trekking in Norway 45

Water sports and adventure in Norwegian waters 48

The main tourist attractions of Norway 50

Oslo: Norway's modern capital 53

Bergen: The charming port city 56

Trondheim: The historic city in central Norway 59

Tromsø: The gateway to the Arctic 62

Stavanger: A city by the sea 64

Kristiansand: The sunny city of the south 66

Norwegian architecture and its influences 68

Traditional Norwegian clothing 70

Norway's rich craftsmanship 72

The music and dances of Norway 74

Norway's most important festivals and holidays 76

Norwegian Literature and Famous Writers 78

Norwegian Painting and Fine Arts 80

Religion and folklore in Norway 82

The Norwegian language and its peculiarities 84

The importance of Norwegian in the modern world 86

Norwegian dialects and regional differences 89

The Norwegian education and higher education system 91

The Norwegian Government and Political Structure 93

Norway's social system and health care system 95

Sustainability and environmental protection in Norway 97

The Norwegian economy and industry 99

Norway's role in the international community 101

Epilogue 103

The geographical location of Norway

Norway's geographical location is of paramount importance for understanding this fascinating country. Norway stretches along the Scandinavian peninsula in northern Europe and borders the Atlantic Ocean to the west. To the east, it is bordered by Sweden, while to the north and northeast runs the country's border with Finland and Russia. This geographical location makes Norway a country of extraordinary diversity and beauty.

Norway's coastline stretches for an impressive 25,000 kilometers, making it one of the longest coastal areas in the world. This vast coastal area is characterized by numerous fjords, bays and islands that form the characteristic landscape of Norway. One of the most famous fjords is the Geirangerfjord, which is lined with steep cliffs and roaring waterfalls and is a UNESCO World Heritage Site.

Inland, majestic mountain ranges rise, including the famous mountain range of the Norwegian Alps, which stretches across large parts of the country. The highest peak in Norway is Galdhøpiggen, which rises an impressive 2,469 meters above sea level. This imposing mountain landscape attracts hikers, mountaineers and nature lovers from all over the world.

Norway is also known for its unique natural phenomena, including the Northern Lights and the Midnight Sun. In the northern regions of Norway, you can watch the impressive spectacle of the Northern Lights in the night sky in winter, while in summer the midnight sun provides daylight for days on end.

Norway's geographical location also has a decisive influence on the country's climate. The coastal regions are influenced by the Gulf Stream, resulting in comparatively mild winters, while the interior has a continental climate with cold winters and warm summers.

Norway's diverse landscape not only has an impact on the climate, but also on the country's wildlife. Norway is home to a wide variety of wildlife, including moose, reindeer, arctic foxes, and whales, which can be found in the waters off the coast.

Overall, Norway's geographical location reflects its uniqueness and beauty. From the majestic fjords to the imposing mountain peaks and the mystical Northern Lights, Norway is undoubtedly a country of remarkable geographical diversity and scenic splendor.

The fascinating history of Norway

Norway's fascinating history is rich in events and turning points that have shaped the development of this Nordic country. The origins of Norwegian history date back to the Viking Age, when these brave navigators ruled the coasts of Norway and explored large parts of Europe. However, Norway, as a country as we know it today, has undergone a long and complex development.

The first human traces in Norway date back to around 10,000 BC, when the first hunter-gatherers arrived in the region. Over the millennia, a distinct culture developed, and in the Bronze Age (around 1800 BC), people began metalworking and building burial mounds.

The Viking Age, which lasted roughly from the 8th to the 11th century, marks one of the most significant periods in Norwegian history. The Vikings from Norway were known for their seafaring skills and conquests that took them in all directions. Under the leadership of famous Vikings such as Erik the Red and Leif Erikson, parts of North America were discovered and settled long before Columbus reached the continent. In the 9th century, the Christianization of Norway began when King Olav Tryggvason introduced Christianity. Later in the 11th century, Norway was forced into a union with Denmark, and a period of Danish rule began.

Norway's aspirations for independence led to the signing of the Grunnloven (Constitution) in 1814, which granted Norway a certain autonomy within the personal union with Sweden. This union lasted until 1905, when Norway declared its independence from Sweden and became its own royal monarchy. During World War II, Norway was occupied by Germany, but resistance from the Norwegian people and the Allies eventually led to the liberation of the country.

Norway's modern history is marked by social democracy, prosperity and a strong focus on environmental protection and sustainability. Norway is known for its welfare systems, education system, and economy based on oil and gas deposits, as well as a strong shipping industry.

The history of Norway is marked by wars, conquests, independence efforts and an impressive development towards a modern and prosperous country. It reflects the struggles and successes of a people who have played a unique role in the history of Europe and the world.

The origins of Norwegian culture

The origins of Norwegian culture go far back in history and are closely linked to the indigenous populations that inhabited the territory of Norway. These cultures left their mark in the form of customs, traditions and ways of life that continue to shape Norwegian identity today.

One of the oldest cultures that can be traced back to Norway is the Sami people, the indigenous people of northern Scandinavia. The Sami have lived in the Arctic regions of Norway, Sweden, Finland and Russia for thousands of years. They have developed their own unique language, culture and way of life, which is heavily influenced by reindeer herding.

The Vikings, who were active in the 8th to 11th centuries, are one of Norway's best-known cultures and have had a significant influence on Norwegian history. The Vikings were not only feared sailors and warriors, but also gifted craftsmen and traders. They left behind a legacy of art, mythology and legal systems that are still present in Norway today. With the Christianization of Norway in the 10th and 11th centuries, the spread of Christianity began, which brought with it a significant cultural change. The church became a central part of Norwegian society, and Norwegian literature and art began to take up religious themes. In the Middle Ages, Norway was a nation made up of various regions and kingdoms, including Trøndelag, Viken, and Westland. Each of these regions had its own cultural peculiarities and traditions, which can still be seen today in the different dialects and customs of Norway.

Norwegian folk music, also known as "folk music," has deep roots in the country's history. It includes various styles and instruments, including the Hardanger fiddle, a special violin from Norway. This musical tradition is often maintained in conjunction with traditional dances such as the "Springar" or the "Halling".

Norwegian cuisine also reflects the cultural influences that the country has experienced throughout history. Traditional dishes such as lutefisk (dried fish), raspeballer (potato dumplings) and koldtbord (cold buffet) are examples of Norway's culinary diversity.

The origins of Norwegian culture are diverse and rich in traditions that are still alive today. The various influences, from the Sami and the Vikings to Christianization and regional differences, have shaped Norwegian identity, making it a fascinating and multifaceted culture.

The Vikings and their traces in Norway

The Vikings and their traces in Norway are a fascinating chapter of Norwegian history that is inextricably linked to the country's development. The Vikings, who were active in the period between the 8th and 11th centuries, originated in the Scandinavian countries, including Norway, Sweden and Denmark. They were known for their brave seafaring, warrior culture, and impressive trade networks that allowed them to travel as far north as North America and the East.

The Norwegian coast, with its numerous fjords, islands and bays, offered the Vikings ideal conditions for their sea voyages. These seafarers were not only explorers, but also conquerors, traveling to distant lands and establishing settlements. Norwegian Vikings, for example, settled parts of Iceland, the Faroe Islands, Greenland, and the Scottish Islands.

A high point in the history of the Norwegian Vikings was the discovery and settlement of Vinland, a region in North America. Leif Erikson, a Norwegian Viking, is often considered to be the first European explorer of North America. The Vikings left archaeological traces there that prove their presence, including settlement remains and artifacts.

The Vikings were not only warlike, but also culturally active. They developed a unique art and mythology, which is recorded in numerous runic inscriptions and works of art. The best-known literary work from this period is the "Edda", a collection of Norse myths and legends.

The Viking Age in Norway finally ended with the Christianization of the country. King Olav Tryggvason played a crucial role in the introduction of Christianity and the spread of Christianity in Norway. Christianization brought about a change in Norwegian culture, as the old gods and customs were replaced by Christianity.

Nevertheless, the traces of the Vikings in Norway are still visible today. Numerous museums, archaeological finds and historical sites commemorate this important period in Norwegian history. The Vikings and their cultural and historical influences are an integral part of Norwegian identity and a fascinating facet of this country's history.

Norway's independence and modern history

Norway's independence and modern history are marked by a complex sequence of political, social and economic developments. Norway's independence from Denmark and later from Sweden marks an important milestone in the country's modern history.

The period of Danish rule over Norway began in the 14th century and lasted for several centuries. During this period, Norway maintained its autonomy and identity, but also experienced political challenges and conflicts. Danish rule finally ended in 1814, when Denmark was forced to cede Norway to Sweden in the course of the Napoleonic Wars.

This led to the formation of a union between Norway and Sweden, which lasted for 91 years. Under this union, Norway had some autonomy, but retained a common monarchy with Sweden. However, dissatisfaction in Norway with the Union led to tensions and conflicts, which eventually led to Norway's independence in 1905.

On June 7, 1905, the Norwegian parliament declared independence from Sweden, and the

Swedish King Oscar II accepted this decision. Norway elected Prince Carl of Denmark as king and became a sovereign kingdom. This peaceful separation from Sweden marked the beginning of Norway's modern history.

During the First World War, Norway remained neutral, but the economic impact of the war was felt. In the years following the war, Norway experienced a period of economic expansion, largely due to the exploitation of its rich oil and gas reserves. These resources were discovered in the 1960s and 1970s and contributed significantly to the country's economic stability and prosperity.

In Norway's modern history, the country's role in international affairs is also significant. Norway is an active member of the United Nations, NATO and other international organizations. It has gained a reputation as a mediator in conflicts and as a champion of human rights and environmental protection.

Norway's history is marked by political change, economic growth, and a strong emphasis on social democracy and welfare systems. The country has maintained its independence and developed into a modern nation with a strong economy and an active international role.

The breathtaking Norwegian nature

The breathtaking Norwegian nature is of a diversity and beauty that is second to none. Norway, located in the north of Europe, covers an area of about 385,207 square kilometers and is home to a landscape characterized by majestic mountains, deep fjords, pristine forests, vast plateaus, and abundant wildlife.

The mountain ranges of Norway, especially the Norwegian Alps, or "fells", offer spectacular views and hiking opportunities. The highest peak, Galdhøpiggen, rises an impressive 2,469 meters above sea level and attracts mountaineers from all over the world. The mountain landscapes are crisscrossed by numerous hiking trails, offering outdoor enthusiasts endless opportunities to explore nature.

The Norwegian fjords are world-famous and represent one of the country's most impressive geographical features. These deep inlets, carved by glaciers, stretch for thousands of kilometres and offer breathtaking views of high rock faces, waterfalls and crystal clear waters. The Geirangerfjord and the Nærøyfjord are

UNESCO World Heritage Sites and are popular destinations for cruises and nature lovers.

Norway's waterfalls are also impressive and add to the beauty of the landscape. Kjosfossen, Vøringsfossen and Seven Sisters Waterfall are just a few examples of the majestic waterfalls that can be admired in Norway.

Norway's coastline stretches for 25,000 kilometres and is lined with numerous islands and skerries. This coastal wealth offers ideal conditions for water sports such as sailing, kayaking and fishing. The Norwegian North Sea coast is also an important habitat for seals, whales and a variety of bird species.

The polar regions of Norway offer a unique natural phenomenon: the midnight sun in summer and the northern lights in winter. In the northern regions of the country, the sun shines around the clock in summer, while in winter the Northern Lights bathe the sky in magical light.

Norwegian nature is not only beautiful, but also diverse. Norway's wildlife includes moose, reindeer, arctic foxes, whales, and numerous species of birds. National parks and nature reserves protect the country's pristine wilderness and provide opportunities for wildlife viewing and recreation in nature.

National parks and nature reserves in Norway

National parks and nature reserves in Norway form an impressive variety of protected landscapes that preserve the natural beauty of the country and preserve it for future generations. Norway takes nature conservation seriously and has taken a number of measures to protect its unique environment.

One of the most famous national parks in Norway is Jotunheimen National Park. With an area of over 1,140 square kilometers, it is the largest national park in the country and is home to some of Norway's highest peaks, including Galdhøpiggen. A paradise for hikers, mountaineers and nature lovers, the park offers stunning alpine scenery.

Another impressive national park is Rondane National Park, which is the oldest in the country. This park is known for its unique high mountain landscape, where reindeer and other animal species can be observed. The clear mountain lakes and open plateaus make Rondane a popular destination for nature lovers.

The Sør Spitsbergen National Park on Spitsbergen, a group of islands in the far north of Norway, protects an Arctic wilderness of extraordinary beauty. This national park is home to polar bears, walruses, and abundant birdlife. The dramatic glaciers and rugged landscape make it a unique place.

Dovrefjell-Sunndalsfjella National Park is an important habitat for Norway's endangered musk ox population. This park is known for its vast plateaus where you can observe the majestic musk oxen in their natural environment.

Numerous nature reserves in Norway protect special ecosystems and animal species. Vøringsfossen Nature Reserve preserves the impressive waterfall landscape of Vøringsfossen, one of Norway's most famous waterfalls. The Vega Archipelago Nature Reserve on the coast of Norway is an important habitat for birds and has been declared a UNESCO World Heritage Site.

The Norwegian government has imposed strict environmental regulations and protective measures in these areas to ensure that the fragile ecosystems and wildlife are preserved. Nature conservation is a high priority in Norway, and the population is actively involved in the preservation of nature.

National parks and nature reserves are not only important places for conservation, but also popular destinations for tourists who want to experience the unspoiled beauty of the Norwegian countryside. They are an important part of Norway's identity and help preserve and protect the country's unique nature.

Norway's fascinating wildlife

Norway's fascinating wildlife is characterized by extraordinary diversity and beauty. This Nordic country, crisscrossed by impressive mountains, deep fjords and vast forests, provides habitat for a rich wildlife that can be found on the mainland as well as in the coastal waters and Arctic regions.

One of Norway's emblematic animal species is the elk, also known as "elg". Norway is home to one of the largest populations of elk in Europe, and these imposing animals are common in the country's forests. The majestic moose are a common sight for nature enthusiasts and wildlife watchers.

Another characteristic animal of Norway is the reindeer, which is found in the northern regions of the country, especially in Lapland. Reindeer herding is a traditional way of life in these areas, and reindeer play an important role in the lives of the Sami, the indigenous people of northern Norway.

Norway's coastal waters are home to a rich variety of marine species. Whales are common here, including orcas, humpback whales, and minke whales. The Lofoten and Vesterålen Islands are known for their whale watching tours, where tourists have the opportunity to experience these majestic sea creatures in their natural environment.

Norway's birdlife is also impressive. The country's Arctic regions are home to numerous species of birds, including the fulmar, kittiwake, and puffin. The Norwegian fjords provide important breeding grounds for seabirds such as the white-tailed eagle, which is one of the largest birds of prey in Northern Europe.

The Arctic areas of Norway are also home to a variety of mammals, including arctic foxes, lemmings, and reindeer. Polar bears can be found on Spitsbergen and other islands in the Arctic, making Norway one of the few countries in the world where these majestic predators can be seen in the wild.

Norwegian wildlife is not only fascinating, but also an important part of Norwegian culture and identity. The people of Norway are actively involved in the protection and conservation of their unique wildlife and strive to preserve the natural habitats. Norway's wildlife is a treasure worth admiring and protecting.

Norway's culinary diversity

Norway's culinary diversity reflects the country's rich history, geographical location, and natural resources. Norwegian cuisine is characterized by fresh and high-quality ingredients, which often come from the untouched nature of Norway. Here are some notable aspects of Norwegian cuisine:

Fish and seafood play a central role in Norwegian cuisine. Norway is famous for its salmon, which is farmed in the clear waters of the fjords. Norwegian salmon is known worldwide for its quality and taste. Likewise, prawns, cod and haddock are important ingredients in many Norwegian dishes.

Another delicacy from the sea is the stockfish, or "Tørrfisk". This dried fish is a traditional Norwegian food that is often used in stews and soups.

Norway is also known for its variety of wildlife, which is integrated into the country's culinary tradition. Reindeer meat is a delicacy and is often served in dishes such as "raspeballer" (potato dumplings) and "finnbiff" (reindeer goulash). Elk meat is also popular and is made into steaks and goulash.

Norwegian cuisine is characterized by its use of fresh vegetables. Potatoes are a staple food and are prepared in a variety of forms, from mashed potatoes to fried potatoes. Cabbage, carrots, peas, and turnips can also be found in many Norwegian dishes.

Norway is a country of dairy products, and cheese is an important ingredient in many dishes. The "Brunost" or "Gjetost" is a unique Norwegian cheese made from goat's milk and has a sweet, caramel-like taste.

The Norwegian bakery and baking tradition is also remarkable. "Kanelboller" (cinnamon rolls) and "lefse" (thin potato breads) are popular pastries that are often served with coffee.

Another aspect of Norwegian cuisine is the traditional method of smoking and preserving food. Smoked salmon, smoked cod and dried fish are examples of these time-honored techniques.

The culinary diversity of Norway reflects the connection of Norwegians with their nature and tradition. The use of local ingredients and the care of old recipes make Norwegian cuisine a unique and tasty experience that visitors from all over the world can enjoy.

The importance of fish in Norwegian cuisine

The importance of fish in Norwegian cuisine is of paramount importance and reflects Norway's close relationship with the sea and its rich waters. Fish is not only a source of food, but also a central part of Norwegian culture and identity.

Norway is surrounded by a long and rugged coastline crisscrossed by numerous fjords, bays and islands. This unique geographical location has meant that fish and seafood have been an essential part of the Norwegian diet for centuries. Norwegians have a long tradition of fishing, dating back to the Viking Age.

One of the most famous Norwegian fish species is salmon, especially Atlantic salmon. Norway is known worldwide for its high-quality salmon, which is farmed in the clear waters of the fjords. Norwegian salmon is characterized by its rich flavor and delicate texture and is used in a variety of dishes, from smoked salmon to fried salmon steak.

Cod, or "torsk" in Norway, is another important type of fish in Norwegian cuisine. Cod is versatile and is prepared in various forms, from cod fillet to cod cod dumplings. Stockfish, dried cod, is a traditional Norwegian food and has been preserved for centuries.

Prawns, or "reker", are a popular delicacy in Norway and are often served at picnics and celebrations. The Norwegian shrimp fishery is an important economic activity and provides fresh shrimp of high quality.

The importance of fish in Norwegian cuisine also extends to smoked and salted fish species such as mackerel and herring. These fish are commonly used in sandwiches, salads, and stews.

In addition to fisheries, sustainable aquaculture also plays an important role in Norway. Norway is one of the world's largest producers of fish farmed products, including salmon and trout. The Norwegian government sets strict environmental requirements to ensure that aquaculture is operated sustainably and the marine environment is protected.

The importance of fish in Norwegian cuisine reflects the deep appreciation for the country's natural resources. Fish is not only a delicious source of food, but also a symbol of Norwegians' attachment to their maritime environment and cultural tradition.

Famous Norwegian dishes and delicacies

Famous Norwegian dishes and delicacies reflect the diversity of Norwegian cuisine and the use of fresh, local ingredients. These culinary treasures are an important part of Norwegian food culture and are appreciated by locals and visitors alike.

One of the most famous Norwegian dishes is "rakfisk", a traditional Norwegian fish delicacy. Rakfisk is made from fermented fish, often trout or carp, and has an intense flavor. It is often served on flatbreads and is especially popular in the Valdres region.

Another popular dish is "lutefisk", dried fish that is soaked in a lye of water and potassium hydroxide before preparation. Often served with a creamy sauce, pea puree, and bacon, lutefisk is a traditional dish, especially during the Christmas season.

"Koldtbord" is a Norwegian version of the cold buffet and includes a variety of cold dishes, including smoked fish, pickled herrings, ham, cheese and bread. This convivial meal is often served at celebrations and feasts.

Potato dumplings, or "raspballer," are a savory specialty that is often served with butter and a gravy. These dumplings can be prepared with various fillings, such as minced meat or bacon.

A sweet treat in Norway is "skillingsboller", cinnamon rolls covered with a sugar glaze. These pastries are popular with locals and tourists alike and are often enjoyed with a cup of coffee.

Norwegian cuisine also offers an abundance of fish dishes, including "torsketunger," fried cod, and "fiskepudding," a fish pudding. These dishes are examples of the versatility of fish in Norwegian cuisine.

In the northern regions of Norway, such as Lapland, reindeer dishes are common. "Finnebiff", a spicy reindeer goulash, and "Renskav", thin strips of roasted reindeer meat, are typical examples of these regional specialties.

Norwegian cuisine is also known for its cheeses, including the "Brunost" or "Gjetost", a sweet goat cheese, and the "Nøkkelost", a spicy cheese with cloves and cumin.

These famous Norwegian dishes and delicacies reflect the traditions, natural resources and creativity of Norwegian cuisine. They are an important part of the Norwegian identity and invite you to discover the diversity and taste of this fascinating country.

Norwegian beverages and brewing culture

Norwegian beverages and brewing culture reflect the country's rich tradition and unique geographical location. Norway, with its clear waters, clean air and fertile soils, offers ideal conditions for the production of beverages that are both traditional and modern.

A well-known Norwegian drink is the "aquavit", a herbal liquor that has been produced in Norway for centuries. Aquavit is made from potatoes or grains and flavored with various herbs and spices, including dill, cumin, and anise. This aromatic drink is often drunk on festive occasions and is an important part of Norwegian culture.

Beer culture in Norway has experienced a strong upswing in recent years. Norway has a growing number of breweries producing a wide range of beers, including traditional varieties such as Pilsner and Kölsch, as well as creative craft beers with innovative flavors. The Norwegian craft beer scene has become one of the most exciting in Europe.

A special feature in Norway is the "Kornøl", a traditional Norwegian beer made from barley and oats. This beer has a long history and is often brewed in rural areas. It has a characteristic, slightly sweet taste and is often enjoyed at celebrations and festivals.

Another interesting drink from Norway is the "kvass", a slightly alcoholic drink made from fermented bread. Kvass has a refreshing and slightly sour note and is often enjoyed in the summer months.

Norwegians are also known for their coffee consumption, drinking one of the highest amounts of coffee per capita in the world. Coffee is an integral part of Norwegian culture, and coffee breaks, known as "coffee breaks", are an important social moment in the everyday life of Norwegians.

Norway's beverage culture reflects the diversity and quality of the country's natural resources. Whether it's traditional drinks like aquavit and Kornøl or modern craft beers, Norway has a lot to offer when it comes to refreshing and flavorful drinks. This diversity and appreciation for good quality are features of Norwegian beverage culture and contribute to the country's rich culinary experience.

The Art of Smoking and Drying Food

The art of smoking and drying food is deeply rooted in Norway and has a long history that spans centuries. These traditional methods of food preservation have allowed Norwegians to enjoy the fruits of their labor in fishing and agriculture all year round, while making the most of natural resources.

Smoking food is a proven technique that involves exposing food via smoke from burning wood or other materials. The smoke not only serves to preserve the food, but also gives it a unique taste and intense aroma. In Norway, it is mainly fish that is smoked, especially salmon and mackerel. The smoking process can take several days and requires patience and experience.

Another traditional method of food preservation is drying. Dried foods have the advantage that they have a long shelf life and can be easily transported. In Norway, it is mainly fish, such as cod and haddock, that is dried. The drying process is often carried out in the fresh air, with the fish being placed on special racks or wooden racks.

Stockfish is a well-known specialty of Norway and is made from dried cod. The cod is dried outdoors on wooden racks, developing its characteristic hard texture in the process. Stockfish is a versatile ingredient in many Norwegian dishes, from stews to soups.

In addition to fish, meat and venison are also dried in Norway. Reindeer meat and elk meat are often made into jerky, a type of dried meat. This dried meat is a protein-rich and energy-rich food and is well suited for hikes and expeditions into the Norwegian wilderness.

The art of smoking and drying food requires not only expertise in the right techniques, but also the selection of high-quality ingredients. The quality of the wood, salt and other spices plays a crucial role in the process of food preservation.

These traditional methods are not only an important culinary tradition in Norway, but also an expression of Norwegians' attachment to their history and natural environment. They show people's ability to adapt to nature's challenges while producing delicious and durable food. The art of smoking and drying food is a valuable part of Norwegian culture and a heritage that is carefully nurtured and passed on.

Norway's impressive fjords

Norway's impressive fjords are a prominent geographical feature of the country and are among the most beautiful and impressive natural wonders in the world. These deep waterways, often surrounded by steep mountains, are a stunning example of Norway's geological history and offer spectacular views that attract visitors from all over the world.

Fjords are elongated valleys formed by glaciers that extend into the sea. Norway is known for its numerous fjords, some of which are among the longest and deepest in the world. One of Norway's most famous fjords is the Geirangerfjord, which is surrounded by steep, snow-capped mountain peaks and is a UNESCO World Heritage Site.

The Sognefjord is the longest fjord in Norway and stretches for more than 200 kilometres. Its impressive length and depth make it a popular destination for cruises and boat trips. The Nærøyfjord, a tributary of the Sognefjord, is also protected as a UNESCO World Heritage Site and offers spectacular scenery.

The Hardangerfjord is another impressive fjord known for its fertile orchards and picturesque villages. This fjord is an important part of Norway's cultural landscape and is often visited by tourists who want to experience the natural beauty and rich history of the region.

The coastline of Norway is crisscrossed by a variety of fjords, including the Lysefjord, which is known for its imposing rock Preikestolen (the pulpit) and the Kjeragbolten, a huge stone enclosed between two rocks.

Fjords offer not only breathtaking views, but also a rich flora and fauna. Many fjords are home to seals, seabirds, and even whales that forage in the waters.

Norway's impressive fjords are a treasure of nature and an important part of Norway's identity. They attract nature lovers, adventurers, and travelers from all over the world who want to experience the majestic landscapes and tranquility of these unique waterways. Norway's fjords are an indispensable element of Norway's landscape and culture, reflecting the beauty and diversity of this fascinating country.

The majestic Norwegian mountains

The majestic Norwegian mountains characterize the country's landscape in an impressive way and are a central element of Norwegian geography and culture. These imposing mountain ranges span much of Norway and provide a stunning backdrop for outdoor activities, nature exploration, and adventure.

One of Norway's most famous mountains is undoubtedly the Trolltunga, or "Troll's Tongue", a rocky outcrop that rises about 700 metres above Lake Ringedalsvatnet. This iconic landmark is a popular destination for hikers and adventurers seeking the thrill of standing on this impressive rock and taking in the spectacular views.

Romsdalseggen Mountain in the Møre og Romsdal region offers one of Norway's most impressive panoramas. From this mountaintop, hikers can enjoy stunning views of the surrounding fjords, valleys, and peaks.

At 2,469 meters, Galdhøpiggen is the highest mountain in Norway and one of the highest in all of Scandinavia. This majestic mountain is located in the Jotunheimen National Park and is a popular destination for mountaineers and hikers.

The Lofoten Islands, a group of islands off the coast of Norway, are known for their dramatic mountain landscapes and pointed rock formations. Here, visitors can admire the contrasts between the deep blue sea and the soaring mountains.

Preikestolen, or "Sermon Chair", is another famous mountain in Norway and offers spectacular views of the Lysefjord. This striking rock rises around 604 meters above the fjord and attracts thousands of visitors who dare to climb to experience the view.

The Norwegian mountains are not only a paradise for hikers and mountaineers, but also for skiers and snowboarders. In the winter months, the snow-capped peaks offer first-class skiing and descent opportunities for winter sports enthusiasts.

The majestic Norwegian mountains are not only a scenic attraction, but also an important part of Norwegian culture and history. They are home to a rich flora and fauna, including reindeer, arctic foxes and mountain hares. The mountains have also shaped the way of life and traditions of the Norwegian people, who have lived in these stunning landscapes for generations.

A symbol of the beauty and wildness of Norway's nature, the Norwegian mountains invite visitors to explore and experience the wonders of these majestic peaks. They are a treasure of the country that impressively reflects the diversity and natural wonders of Norway.

Norway's unparalleled waterfalls

Norway's incomparable waterfalls are an impressive manifestation of the country's natural beauty and another fascinating element of its spectacular scenery. These waterfalls, of which there are hundreds in Norway, are a testament to the geographical diversity and amounts of water that can be found in this Nordic country.

Vøringsfossen is one of Norway's most famous waterfalls and a popular destination for tourists. With a drop of about 182 meters, the water plunges spectacularly into a deep gorge and forms an impressive sight. The viewing platforms at Vøringsfossen offer breathtaking views of this majestic waterfall.

Steinsdalsfossen near Norheimsund is a special waterfall that allows visitors to step behind the falling veil of water. A path leads directly behind the waterfall, which offers a unique experience and gives the opportunity to admire the waterfall from a unique perspective.

Kjosfossen, along the famous Flåm Railway route, is another spectacular waterfall. This waterfall cascades down from the surrounding mountains with great force, creating an impressive murmur that makes the ride on the Flåm Railway an unforgettable experience.

The Tvindefossen near Voss is a waterfall of great beauty and importance. It plunges into a picturesque lake in two mighty cascades, providing an idyllic backdrop for nature lovers and photographers.

In addition to the well-known waterfalls, there are numerous others in Norway that impress with their natural splendor and wildness. Waterfalls such as Hengjane, Langfossen, Månafossen and Rjukanfossen are examples of the diversity and beauty of Norwegian waterfalls.

The waterfalls of Norway are not only spectacular natural phenomena, but also an important part of Norwegian culture and history. They are sources of inspiration for art, literature and legends and have captured people's imaginations over the centuries.

Norway's incomparable waterfalls are a treasure of nature and a reflection of the country's diversity and beauty. They are a fascinating element of the Norwegian landscape and invite you to discover and admire the wonders of these majestic water features.

The Northern Lights: The Magical Spectacle of the Sky

The Northern Lights, also known as the Aurora Borealis, are undoubtedly one of the most fascinating and magical natural phenomena the sky has to offer. In Norway, especially in the northern regions of the country, you have the opportunity to experience this breathtaking spectacle of the sky in all its glory.

The Northern Lights are formed by the interaction of charged particles from the Sun, known as the solar wind, with the gases in the Earth's atmosphere. These particles get close to the poles, where they meet the gases in the atmosphere, especially oxygen and nitrogen. During this collision, the gases emit light, creating the vivid and colorful appearances of the Northern Lights.

In Norway, the best chances to see the Northern Lights are during the dark winter months from September to March. During this time, the skies in the northern regions of the country are often clear and free of distracting light, creating ideal conditions for Northern Lights viewing.

One of the best places in Norway to see the Northern Lights is Tromsø. This city is located in the Arctic region of Norway and is often referred to as the "Capital of the Northern Lights". There are numerous opportunities to take part in guided Northern Lights tours here, increasing the chances of experiencing this spectacular phenomenon.

The colors of the Northern Lights can vary from green to pink, purple and even red. The intensity and shape of the Northern Lights can also vary, ranging from gentle arches to vibrant waves and curtains that sweep the entire sky.

The Northern Lights have always played a special role in Norwegian culture and history. In ancient times, people believed that the Northern Lights were the souls of the deceased or that they brought messages from another world. Today, the Northern Lights are an important part of tourism in Norway and attract travelers from all over the world who want to experience this unique natural phenomenon.

The Northern Lights are undoubtedly a magical spectacle of the sky and an impressive testimony to the wonders of nature. They are a symbol of the unique beauty and magic of Norwegian nature, offering those who experience them unforgettable and touching moments under the star-studded skies of the far north.

The Midnight Sun: Norway's Endless Days in Summer

The midnight sun, also known as "Midnattssol" in Norwegian, is a fascinating and unique natural phenomenon that Norway experiences during the summer months. It is a sign of the geographical location of the country, which stretches far to the north, and of the tilt of the Earth's axis. During this time, the sun does not sink below the horizon, and the days are endless, with uninterrupted daylight.

The midnight sun occurs in Norway mainly in the northern regions above the Arctic Circle. This phenomenon can be observed during the period of the so-called "white summer", when the nights are as bright as the days. The exact dates vary depending on your geographical location, with the period peaking around the summer solstice at the end of June.

Tromsø, the largest city in northern Norway, is a popular place to experience the midnight sun. The city organizes numerous events and festivals to celebrate this unique natural phenomenon and attracts tourists from all over the world.

The Midnight Sun has a deep cultural and historical influence on Norway. It has shaped the way of life of people in the northern regions of the country and has often been captured in art, literature and music. The midnight sun symbolizes the beauty and uniqueness of Norwegian nature and people's ability to adapt to extreme environmental conditions.

During the time of the midnight sun, Norway offers a variety of outdoor activities and adventures that take advantage of the uninterrupted daylight. This ranges from midnight kayaking to mountain hikes in the brightest daylight.

The Midnight Sun is undoubtedly one of Norway's most amazing natural phenomena and an experience that captivates every visitor. It is a tribute to the stunning nature of Norway and a testament to the amazing diversity and beauty of this Nordic country. The endless days in summer that the midnight sun brings are a time of joy and celebration where people can experience the splendor of nature in its full glory.

The best places for hiking and trekking in Norway

Norway is undoubtedly a paradise for outdoor enthusiasts and hiking lovers. With its diverse and stunning scenery, the country offers an abundance of opportunities for hiking and trekking, ranging from gentle coastal walks to challenging mountain treks.

One of the most famous places for hiking in Norway is Rondane National Park, the oldest national park in the country. Here, visitors can explore pristine wilderness, mountain lakes, and majestic peaks. The Rondane offers numerous hiking trails of varying difficulty that allow hikers to fully enjoy the beauty of nature.

Jotunheimen National Park is another spectacular place for hiking and trekking. It is home to Norway's highest mountain, Galdhøpiggen, which can be climbed by experienced mountaineers. The park also offers numerous well-marked hiking trails that pass through alpine landscapes, valleys, and glaciers.

The Lofoten Islands, a group of islands in northern Norway, are known for their dramatic mountain landscapes and offer excellent hiking opportunities along the coastline and in the mountains. The hiking trails in Lofoten offer breathtaking views of the sea and the surrounding islands.

In the Telemark region of southern Norway, hikers will find the famous Telemark Canal, which winds through a picturesque landscape of lakes, rivers and forests. The surrounding forests also offer excellent opportunities for hiking and the chance to experience unspoiled nature.

Dovrefjell-Sunndalsfjella National Park is a great place to explore the Norwegian wilderness and spot wildlife such as reindeer and musk oxen. The diverse hiking trails in this national park lead through alpine tundra landscapes and offer unique nature experiences.

The Norwegian fjords, including the Nærøyfjord and the Geirangerfjord, also offer impressive opportunities for hiking along their shores and slopes. These regions are characterized by steep mountains, deep fjords and abundant wildlife.

Norway offers hiking and trekking opportunities for adventurers of all levels, from beginners to experienced mountaineers. The country's landscapes are diverse and spectacular, and the nature experiences that can be enjoyed while hiking in Norway are unforgettable.

The best places for hiking and trekking in Norway are characterized by an impressive variety of landscapes, from mountains and fjords to forests and coasts. Whether you are looking for the challenge of a summit climb or just want to experience the tranquility of nature, Norway has a wealth of options for hiking enthusiasts.

Water sports and adventure in Norwegian waters

Water sports and adventure in Norwegian waters are an exciting aspect of life and tourism in Norway. The country, which stretches from the coast of the Atlantic Ocean and the North Sea to its numerous fjords, lakes and rivers, offers a rich variety of opportunities for water sports enthusiasts and adventure seekers.

One of the most popular activities in Norway's waters is kayaking. The country's coastline is lined with countless islands, bays, and fjords that provide ideal conditions for kayakers. From calm coastal waters to wilder sea passages, Norway offers a variety of opportunities for kayaking adventures.

Sailing is another popular water sport in Norway. The country's numerous fjords and lakes offer excellent conditions for sailors who want to explore the picturesque coastline. The Norwegian fjords, including the Geirangerfjord and the Lysefjord, are popular sailing destinations.

Fishing is also a widespread recreational activity in Norway and attracts anglers from all over the world. Norwegian waters are rich in fish stocks, including salmon, trout, cod and halibut. Rivers such as the Orkla, the Gaula and the Namsen are particularly popular with fly fishers.

For those looking for a dose of adrenaline, Norway's waters also offer opportunities for extreme sports such as white water rafting and kitesurfing. The vicinity of Voss is home to some of Norway's best whitewater rafting routes, while the coastal regions offer ideal conditions for kitesurfing.

Diving is another exciting activity in Norwegian waters. Norway is known for its clear waters and rich marine life. Wrecks, underwater caves and coral reefs attract divers from all over the world.

Norwegian waters are also a haven for nature lovers and wildlife watchers. Whales, dolphins and seals can be spotted off the coast, while birdwatchers appreciate the abundant birdlife in the coastal areas.

Water sports and adventures in Norwegian waters offer a wealth of opportunities to experience the beauty and diversity of Norwegian nature. Whether you're paddling on calm lakes, rafting in wild rivers, or diving in clear waters, Norway has something for every water sports enthusiast and adventure seeker.

The main tourist attractions of Norway

Norway's main tourist attractions are as diverse as the stunning scenery of the country itself. Norway offers visitors a wealth of things to see and do, ranging from the majestic fjords and mountains to the vibrant cities and cultural treasures.

One of Norway's outstanding highlights is its impressive fjords. The Geirangerfjord and the Nærøyfjord, both UNESCO World Heritage Sites, offer spectacular views of steep rock faces, sparkling waters and majestic waterfalls. A boat trip through these fjords is an unforgettable experience.

The city of Bergen is one of Norway's top tourist attractions and a cultural hub of the country. The historic old town of Bryggen with its colourful wooden houses is a popular destination for visitors. Bergen is also the starting point for trips to the fjords and the surrounding mountains.

Norway's capital, Oslo, offers a wealth of attractions, including the impressive Opera House, the Viking Ship Museum, and

Vigeland Park, which houses the sculptures of sculptor Gustav Vigeland. The Munch Museum, dedicated to the famous painter Edvard Munch, is also a popular attraction.

The Northern Lights, also known as the Aurora Borealis, attract thousands of tourists to northern Norway every year. Places like Tromsø offer optimal conditions to experience this fascinating natural phenomenon.

The city of Trondheim is famous for its imposing Nidaros Cathedral and its historic old town. It is also an important starting point for trips to the Norwegian fjords and mountains.

The Lofoten Islands, a group of islands off the coast of Norway, are a paradise for nature lovers and adventurers. The dramatic mountain landscapes, quaint fishing villages, and the opportunity to spot whales and seabirds make Lofoten a unique destination.

Norway's national parks, including Rondane National Park, Jotunheimen National Park and Dovrefjell-Sunndalsfjella National Park, offer ample opportunities for hiking, trekking and exploring unspoiled nature.

Norway's coastline stretches for thousands of kilometres and offers plenty of opportunities for coastal walks, boat trips and water sports activities.

The Sami culture in Norway offers visitors the opportunity to experience the unique culture and traditions of the Sami, the country's indigenous people. The Sami National Museum in Karasjok and the Sami Art Centre in Kautokeino are important points of contact.

Norwegian cuisine, with its fresh seafood, salmon, reindeer meat, and traditional dishes such as lutefisk and raspeballer, is a culinary experience that many tourists enjoy.

Norway's main tourist attractions offer an impressive mix of natural beauty, cultural treasures and outdoor activities. Whether you want to explore the majestic nature, visit historic cities or taste the country's culinary delights, Norway has something for everyone.

Oslo: Norway's modern capital

Oslo, the modern capital of Norway, is a city that masterfully manages the balancing act between urban lifestyle and natural beauty. This lively metropolis on the Oslo Fjord has a lot to offer and is a major cultural and economic centre of Norway.

The city of Oslo was first founded in the 11th century and has a rich history dating back to the Viking Age. Today, it is a modern and cosmopolitan city, known for its high quality of life and progressive design.

One of Oslo's most notable sights is the Opera House, an architectural masterpiece located on the harbor that looks like a floating iceberg ship. Visitors can climb to the top of the impressive rooftop terrace and enjoy stunning views of the city and fjord from there.

Vigeland Park is another of Oslo's cultural treasures. Home to more than 200 life-size sculptures by sculptor Gustav Vigeland, this sculpture park is a place of rest and contemplation.

The Munch Museum is dedicated to the famous Norwegian painter Edvard Munch and houses an impressive collection of his works, including the famous painting "The Scream". Munch's works are an important part of Norwegian art history, and the museum offers a fascinating insight into his work.

Oslo also offers a diverse gastronomic scene, from traditional Norwegian cuisine to international delicacies. Aker Brygge is a popular harbourside neighbourhood where restaurants, bars and shops stretch along the waterfront, providing a lively ambience.

The city is also a major economic hub of Norway and is home to numerous businesses, including oil and gas companies, technology companies, and financial institutions. Oslo's economic power contributes to the country's stability and prosperity.

Nature is always present, even in an urban environment like Oslo. The nearby Oslo Fjord and the surrounding forests offer numerous opportunities for outdoor activities such as hiking, cycling and water sports. Being close to nature is an important part of the lifestyle in Oslo.

Oslo is also a city of knowledge and education, with renowned universities and research institutions. The high level of educational participation and innovation are characteristic of the city and contribute to its dynamism.

The modern capital of Norway, Oslo is a city that combines its rich history with a forward-thinking approach. With its mix of culture, nature, business and education, Oslo has a lot to offer and is an exciting destination for visitors from all over the world.

Bergen: The charming port city

Bergen, the charming port city of Norway, is a unique place rich in history and beauty. Located on the western shore of Norway on the Bergensfjord, this picturesque town has developed over the centuries into a major commercial and cultural centre.

Bergen's history dates back to the time of the Hanseatic League, when the city was an important trading post for the trade in fish and other goods. Traces of this past can still be found in the historic old town of Bryggen, which is a UNESCO World Heritage Site. The colourful wooden houses along Bryggen's quay houses are a characteristic feature of the town and offer a glimpse into Bergen's rich history.

Another outstanding feature of Bergen is its stunning natural environment. The city is surrounded by seven mountains, including Fløyen and Ulriken, which offer plenty of opportunities for hikers and outdoor enthusiasts. The views from the tops of these mountains are spectacular, offering panoramic views of the city and the fjord.

The Bergenhus Fortress Complex is a historic landmark that takes visitors back to Bergen's medieval history. The fortress is home to the Rosenkrantz Tower, Haakon's Hall, and Bergenhus Castle, all of which offer a glimpse into the city's past.

Bergen is also known for its vibrant cultural scene. The Edvard Grieg Museum, dedicated to the famous Norwegian composer, and the KODE Art Museum are important cultural institutions in the city. In addition, there are numerous theatres, concert halls and festivals that take place throughout the year.

The fish hall, also known as "Fisketorget", is a popular spot for foodies, offering fresh seafood and local specialties. Here, visitors can sample Norwegian salmon, crab, fish soups, and more.

The lively Bryggen Wharf harbour promenade offers shopping, restaurants and bars overlooking the harbour. Here, visitors can soak up the maritime atmosphere of the city and shop for souvenirs.

Bergen is also an important starting point for trips to the Norwegian fjords and offers boat tours through the Geirangerfjord and the

Nærøyfjord, two of Norway's most beautiful fjords.

The charming port city of Bergen is a fascinating blend of history, culture and natural beauty. Its rich past, stunning surroundings, and lively atmosphere make it an unforgettable destination for visitors from all over the world.

Trondheim: The historic city in central Norway

Trondheim, the historic city in central Norway, is a place of great importance in Norwegian history and culture. The city, located on the banks of the Nidelva River, has a long and rich past dating back to the Viking Age.

The history of Trondheim is closely linked to the Norwegian monarchy. The city was once the capital of Norway and the place where Norwegian kings were crowned. Nidaros Cathedral, also known as Nidaros Cathedral, is the city's most recognizable landmark and served as a coronation church for Norwegian kings. The imposing Gothic cathedral is an impressive architectural feat and an important place of pilgrimage.

In addition to the Nidaros Cathedral, the Archbishop's Palace is also a historic building of great importance. It was once the seat of the Archbishop of Norway and is now a museum that presents the history of the city and the Norwegian Church.

Trondheim's Old Town, also known as Bakklandet, is a picturesque neighbourhood with narrow streets, colourful wooden houses and a lively atmosphere. Here you will find cosy cafés, restaurants and shops that invite you to stroll and linger.

The city is also home to the Norwegian University of Science and Technology (NTNU), a renowned educational institution and center for research and innovation. Trondheim is an important educational location in Norway and attracts students from home and abroad.

The river promenade along the Nidelva is a popular place to walk and relax. Here you can admire the historic wooden bridges that cross the river and enjoy the view of the old town.

Trondheim is also known for its cultural scene, with theatres, concert halls and museums, including Trøndelag Teater, Trondheim Symfoniorkester and Trondheim Art Museum. The city offers a rich cultural offer throughout the year.

The surroundings of Trondheim are characterized by impressive nature, with forests, lakes and rivers ideal for hiking, cycling and fishing. The proximity to the coast also allows for water sports activities such as sailing and kayaking.

Trondheim, the historic city in central Norway, is a place that combines history, culture and nature. Its importance in Norwegian history, vibrant cultural scene, and picturesque surroundings make it a delightful destination for visitors who want to experience the diversity of Norway.

Tromsø: The gateway to the Arctic

Tromsø, the gateway to the Arctic, is a city of special importance in northern Norway. It is located on the island of Tromsøya and is one of the northernmost cities in the world. Tromsø's location in the Arctic makes it a unique and fascinating destination.

The history of Tromsø dates back to the 13th century, when the city served as a trading post and starting point for Arctic expeditions. Today, Tromsø is a modern city known for its scientific facilities and its role as a center for Arctic research.

One of Tromsø's most recognizable landmarks is the Arctic Cathedral, a modern church known for its striking architecture and glass façade. The cathedral is both a religious and cultural center and offers concerts and cultural events throughout the year.

The city is also home to the Polar Museum, which sheds light on the history of polar exploration and the challenges of life in the Arctic. Visitors can learn more about the famous polar explorers such as Roald Amundsen and Fridtjof Nansen.

Tromsø is also a popular starting point for Northern Lights viewing. Due to its location in the Arctic Circle, the city offers optimal conditions for experiencing this fascinating natural phenomenon. Tourists flock to the city during the winter months to admire the aurora borealis in the night sky.

The surroundings of Tromsø offer numerous outdoor activities, including dog sledding, snowmobile tours and skiing. The nearby Lyngen Alps are a popular destination for skiers and snowboarders.

The city is also a major port for expedition cruises to the Arctic, offering the opportunity to spot the region's unique wildlife, including polar bears, whales, and reindeer.

Tromsø is a vibrant and diverse city that, despite its remote location in the Arctic, is an important hub for research, culture and tourism. Its unique position and rich history make it an unforgettable destination for adventurers and explorers.

Stavanger: A city by the sea

Stavanger, a city by the sea, is located on the southwest coast of Norway and is one of the most important cities in the region. This historic town has evolved over the centuries from a small fishing village to an important economic and cultural center.

The history of Stavanger dates back to the Middle Ages, when the city was an important trading port for fish and other goods. Traces of this past can still be found in the well-preserved old town of Stavanger. The colorful wooden houses, narrow alleys and cobblestone streets give the town a charming and historic character.

A standout feature of Stavanger is the Norwegian Oil Capital, as the city is the center of Norway's oil and gas industry. The oil discoveries in the North Sea in the 1960s have made Stavanger an important hub for oil production and exploration. The Norwegian Oil Museum in Stavanger offers insights into the history and importance of this industry for Norway.

Stavanger Cathedral, also known as Stavanger domkirke, is one of Norway's oldest cathedrals and a significant religious building. It dates back to the 12th century and is an impressive example of medieval architecture.

Stavanger is also known for its vibrant cultural scene. The city is home to the Stavanger Concert Hall, the Stavanger Art Museum and the Rogaland Teater, all of which offer a wide range of cultural events and activities.

The surroundings of Stavanger are characterized by breathtaking natural beauty. The region offers numerous opportunities for outdoor activities such as hiking, fishing and water sports. The nearby Lysefjord is a popular destination for tourists and is home to famous sights such as the Preikestolen (Preacher's Chair) and the Kjeragbolten.

The city of Stavanger is also known for its culinary scene, which includes fresh seafood and local specialties such as "Rakfisk" and "Lutefisk". Restaurants and cafes along the harbour promenade offer delicious dishes overlooking the sea.

Stavanger, a city by the sea, combines history, culture and nature in a fascinating way. Its importance as the oil capital of Norway, its rich history and its stunning surroundings make it an exciting destination for visitors from all over the world.

Kristiansand: The sunny city of the south

Kristiansand, the sunny city of the south, is located on the south coast of Norway and is a city of special beauty and diversity. The seaside location, mild climate and rich nature make Kristiansand a popular destination for locals and tourists alike.

The history of Kristiansand dates back to the 17th century, when the town was founded by King Christian IV of Denmark and Norway. The name of the city is derived in his honor. Kristiansand's historic centre, Posebyen, is one of Norway's best-preserved old towns and is characterised by its narrow streets and well-preserved wooden houses.

Kristiansand also has an important port, which is an important hub for trade and fishing. Kristiansand's harbour area offers a lively atmosphere with restaurants, shops and events.

One of the most famous attractions in Kristiansand is Kristiansand Dyrepark. This park is the largest of its kind in Norway and features a variety of animals, including lions, giraffes, and penguins. The amusement park area offers fun and entertainment for the whole family. The surroundings of Kristiansand are characterized by breathtaking nature. The coast near the town offers beautiful beaches, including the popular Bystranda beach. The archipelago and islands off the coast are ideal destinations for boat trips and water sports activities.

The climate in Kristiansand is comparatively mild, which makes the city a popular destination for summer vacationers. The long summer season allows for outdoor activities such as hiking, cycling and fishing.

Kristiansand is also culturally active, with theatres, concert halls and museums, including the Kristiansand Art Museum and the Sørlandets Art Museum, which present an impressive collection of Norwegian art.

The town also has a culinary scene that includes fresh seafood and local specialties such as "Sørlandschips" and "Pølse med lompe". The restaurants in Kristiansand offer a variety of taste experiences for visitors.

Kristiansand, the sunny city of the south, offers a mix of history, nature, culture and entertainment. The relaxed atmosphere and variety of activities make it a delightful destination that has something for everyone.

Norwegian architecture and its influences

Norwegian architecture reflects the country's rich history, unique nature, and cultural diversity. It has been shaped by various influences over the centuries and has become a multifaceted and fascinating form of expression.

Early Norwegian architecture was strongly influenced by Nordic and Viking traditions. The Vikings left traces in the form of stave churches, which are considered one of Norway's most characteristic architectural styles. These wooden churches, which were often decorated with intricate carvings, are a significant cultural heritage and some of them still stand in different parts of Norway.

During the Middle Ages, Romanesque and Gothic influences came into Norwegian architecture, especially in the construction of churches and cathedrals. Nidaros Cathedral in Trondheim is an outstanding example of Gothic architecture and served as the coronation church of the Norwegian kings.

The Renaissance brought Italian influences to Norwegian architecture in the 16th century, which manifested themselves in representative buildings and castles. The baroque and classicist architecture that became popular in the 18th century can also be found in Norway.

Modernism and functionalism influenced Norwegian architecture in the 20th century. Norway became an important venue for architectural experimentation and innovation. Well-known architects such as Arnstein Arneberg and Magnus Poulsson shaped this era with their designs and buildings.

More recently, Norwegian architecture has gained international recognition, especially for innovative buildings and sustainable design concepts. Norway is also known for its modern timber construction, which takes up and develops the traditional use of wood in architecture.

A notable example of contemporary Norwegian architecture is the Oslo Opera House, a spectacular building that rises on the waterfront and has a unique architectural form.

Norwegian architecture reflects the country's values and identity, while at the same time meeting the challenges of the modern world. It is a multifaceted expression of tradition, innovation and the country's relationship with nature.

Traditional Norwegian clothing

Traditional Norwegian clothing reflects the country's long history, climatic conditions, and cultural diversity. It has evolved over the centuries and has given rise to various regional variations.

Norway has a cool climate, especially in the northern regions, and traditional clothing has been designed to provide warmth and protection from the elements. One of the most famous pieces of clothing is the "Bunad", a festive traditional dress that is worn in different variations in different regions of Norway. The bunad is often made of wool and is elaborately embroidered and decorated with silver buttons. It is worn on special occasions such as weddings, festivals and national holidays.

The Sami, the indigenous people of northern Norway, have their own traditional clothing tailored to the needs of life in the Arctic tundra. The "Gákti" is a Sami garment made of leather, wool and other natural materials. They are often intricately decorated with traditional patterns and colors.

In the coastal regions of Norway, fishing was an important source of income, and fishermen wore special clothing to protect themselves from wind and water. The "East Frisian jacket" is an example of such fisherman's clothing, which was worn in some parts of Norway.

Wool sweaters, such as the famous "Norwegian sweater" or "Lusekofte," are also a characteristic piece of clothing in Norway. Warm and sturdy, these sweaters were traditionally worn by fishermen and farmers. They are often decorated with traditional patterns that represent the wearer's region or family.

Traditional Norwegian clothing has a close connection to the culture and history of the country. It shows the craftsmanship of the Norwegians and how they deal with the challenges of the Nordic climate. Despite the modernization and influence of global fashion, traditional clothing remains an important part of the Norwegian identity and is often worn on special occasions and celebrations.

Norway's rich craftsmanship

Norway's rich craftsmanship is a fascinating aspect of the country's culture and history. Over the centuries, Norwegian craftsmen have developed a wide range of skills and techniques that are used in various fields, from wood carving to textile art.

One of the most well-known forms of Norwegian craftsmanship is wood carving. This art has deep roots in Norwegian history and has traditionally been used to create religious artifacts, furniture, and building decorations. Wood carving from Norway is often characterized by detailed and filigree patterns that reflect the craftsmanship and skill of the artists. Norway's famous stave churches are an impressive example of this tradition.

Another important form of Norwegian craftsmanship is textile production. Norway is known for its traditional knitting patterns and techniques, which can be found in wool sweaters, scarves, and blankets. The famous "Norwegian sweater" or "Lusekofte" is known worldwide and features intricate patterns and designs that often reflect regional differences and cultural elements.

The Sami, the indigenous people of northern Norway, have their own rich craft tradition. Her intricately crafted objects, such as the "Sámi art", are made of leather, pearls and silver and are often inspired by nature and its way of life.

Traditional boatbuilding also has a long history in Norway. The "Nordlandboat" and the "Hardangerjakt" are examples of Norwegian boats that have been made with great care and craftsmanship. These boats have been used for both fishing and transport and are an important part of Norway's maritime culture.

Norway's rich craftsmanship reflects the country's close connection to nature and history. It is an expression of creativity, tradition and craftsmanship that continues to be appreciated and nurtured today. Norway's artisans continue these traditions and help preserve and enrich the country's unique culture.

The music and dances of Norway

Norway's music and dances are steeped in a rich and diverse tradition that reflects the country's history, culture and nature. This traditional music and accompanying dances have evolved over the centuries and are an important part of Norwegian identity.

Norwegian folk music, also known as "folk music", is rich in melodies and rhythms, often inspired by nature and rural ways of life. One of the most well-known forms of Norwegian folk music is the "Hardingfele" or Hardanger fiddle, a special form of violin known for its unique sound and elaborate decoration. This violin is often played in traditional dances and festivals.

The "Gammeldans" is a form of traditional Norwegian dance that is danced to the sounds of folk music. The dances vary by region and include steps and figures that have been passed down from generation to generation. At many festivals and celebrations in Norway, these traditional dances are performed and enjoyed by people of all ages.

The Norwegian music scene has also absorbed modern influences, producing many talented musicians and bands that have achieved international success. Norway is known for its diverse musical landscape, ranging from classical music to rock, pop, and electronic music. Artists such as Edvard Grieg, A-ha and Kygo have brought Norway's music to the global stage.

The nature of Norway has a strong influence on the country's music. The expansive landscapes, majestic mountains and rushing waterfalls have inspired musicians and composers, leading to works that capture the beauty and atmosphere of nature.

Overall, the music and dances of Norway are a living expression of Norwegian culture and history. They are a source of joy and pride for the people of Norway and invite visitors to participate in the country's rich musical tradition. The diversity and depth of Norwegian music and dances reflect the rich culture and vibrant soul of Norway.

Norway's most important festivals and holidays

Norway's most significant festivals and holidays are an important facet of Norwegian culture, offering insights into the country's traditions, customs, and celebrations. These special occasions are often marked by a mix of historical, religious and cultural elements.

One of the most famous festivals in Norway is the National Day on May 17th, also known as "Syttende Mai". This day marks Norway's independence from Denmark in 1814 and is a national holiday celebrated with parades, parades, concerts, and feasts. People wear traditional Norwegian costumes, the "bunads", and there is a festive atmosphere throughout the country.

The "Jonsok" or "St. John's Festival" on June 24 is another important festival in Norway. This festival marks the summer solstice and is often celebrated with bonfires, dances, and traditional games. It is also an occasion for people to gather in nature and enjoy the short but intense summer night.

"Jul" or Christmas is an important holiday in Norway that is associated with many traditions and customs. The Norwegian Christmas season begins on December 13 with "Lucia Day", when young girls in white robes and with candles on their heads parade through the streets singing. Christmas preparations include decorating houses and preparing traditional dishes such as 'lutefisk' and 'risengrynsgrøt'. On Christmas Eve, the "Julaften", gifts are exchanged and people gather for Christmas dinner.

The "Påske" or Easter is another important festival in Norway. During the Easter season, Easter bunnies and brightly painted eggs are common. People go to church, spend time in nature and enjoy typical Easter foods such as "Påskeøl" and "Lammekoteletter".

In addition to these festive occasions, there are many local festivals and holidays celebrated in different regions of Norway. These include fishing festivals, music festivals and traditional markets showcasing regional produce and handicrafts.

In Norway, the connection to nature and the country's history comes alive in many festivals and holidays. These occasions are an opportunity for people to celebrate their identity and cultural roots, while also giving visitors an insight into Norway's rich culture. The variety of festivals and holidays reflects the diversity and pride of Norwegian culture.

Norwegian Literature and Famous Writers

Norwegian literature has a long and rich history that spans centuries. It reflects the cultural evolution and identity of the country and has produced an impressive number of talented writers.

One of the earliest known literary works from Norway is the "Edda", a collection of Old Norse mythological and heroic poems. These texts, believed to have been written in the 13th century, are an important heritage of Norwegian literature and have influenced Norse mythology and culture.

In the 19th century, Norwegian literature experienced a boom that was closely linked to the country's national identity and independence movement. An outstanding author of this period was Henrik Ibsen, who is considered one of the most important playwrights in world literature. His works such as "Nora or A Doll's House" and "Ghosts" have had a significant influence on modern theatre and deal with social and psychological issues.

Another important writer of the 19th century was Bjørnstjerne Bjørnson, who received the Nobel Prize for Literature. His work "Synnøve Solbakken" is an example of his novels that reflect the rural culture of Norway and the social changes of the time.

In modern times, Norway has produced a variety of talented authors. The writer Knut Hamsun was also awarded the Nobel Prize for Literature and is known for his novels such as "Hunger" and "Growth of the Soil". His works are characterized by an introspective and psychological approach.

Norwegian literature also has a strong tradition of crime fiction and suspense novels, which has achieved international success. Authors such as Jo Nesbø and Karin Fossum are known for their suspenseful and well-constructed crime novels.

The Norwegian literary landscape is diverse, ranging from poetry and prose to dramas and crime novels. It reflects Norway's history and social changes and contributes to the country's national identity. Norway's famous writers have influenced the literary world and their works continue to be read and appreciated worldwide.

Norwegian Painting and Fine Arts

Norwegian painting and fine arts have a rich history and have produced many talented artists over the centuries. These artworks reflect the culture, nature and identity of Norway and have occupied an important place in the national and international art scene.

One of the most famous periods in Norwegian painting is the so-called "Golden Era", which began in the 19th century. Artists such as Johan Christian Dahl, Adolph Tidemand and Hans Gude were part of this movement, creating landscape paintings that captured the stunning Norwegian nature and landscape. These paintings helped to make the beauty of Norway accessible to a wide public and contributed to the development of national pride.

Another important Norwegian painter of the 19th century was Edvard Munch, who became internationally known for his famous painting "The Scream". Munch is one of the pioneers of Expressionism and his works are known for their emotional intensity and artistic innovation.

In modernism, the Norwegian art scene has produced a wide range of styles and forms of expression. Artists such as Harald Sohlberg and Nikolai Astrup created works inspired by the nature of Norway and the mystical aspects of the landscape. Abstract art also found its place in Norway, with artists such as Inger Sitter and Karel Appel gaining international recognition.

The contemporary Norwegian art scene is diverse and vibrant, and many young artists continue the tradition of innovation and experimentation. Norway has a variety of art museums and galleries, including the Munch Museum in Oslo and the Nasjonalmuseet, which exhibit a wide collection of Norwegian art.

Norwegian painting and visual arts have undergone impressive development throughout history, helping to represent Norway's cultural and artistic diversity. The works of these artists have shaped the national identity and are also internationally appreciated for their quality and originality.

Religion and folklore in Norway

Religion and folklore play a significant role in Norwegian culture and society. Norway has a long religious history, ranging from the Christianization of the country to the modern diversity of faiths. At the same time, Norwegian folklore has deep roots and reflects the country's nature, history and traditions.

The Christianization of Norway began in the 10th century, when King Olav Tryggvason wanted to introduce Christianity. This led to the spread of Christianity in the country, and Norway became a predominantly Christian country in the Middle Ages. The Lutheran denomination dominates the Norwegian Church, and it continues to be an important part of social life.

The Church of Norway has a close connection to the country's history and culture. Many Norwegian holidays and traditions are associated with religious elements, such as Christmas and Easter. The Church of Norway also plays a role in important life events such as baptisms, confirmations, weddings and funerals.

In addition to Christianity, there is a growing diversity of religious beliefs in Norway, including other Christian denominations, Islam, Buddhism, Hinduism, and more. Freedom of religion is protected in Norway, and people have the right to practice their faith.

Norwegian folklore is rich in stories, myths and legends, often associated with nature and the seasons. Elves, trolls and other mythological creatures play an important role in folklore and are part of Norwegian identity. Norwegian folklore also reflects the harsh living conditions in the past and contains many stories about dealing with the forces of nature and the elements.

The Sami, the indigenous population of Norway, have their own religious and folkloric traditions that are closely linked to nature and reindeer herding. This culture has a strong influence on the folklore and cultural diversity of Norway.

Overall, religion and folklore are important elements of Norwegian culture and contribute to the diversity and understanding of the country. They reflect the history, values and identity of Norway and are an important part of the daily lives of the people of this fascinating country.

The Norwegian language and its peculiarities

The Norwegian language is a fascinating element of Norwegian culture and identity. It has its own peculiarities that distinguish it from other languages and reflects the history and diversity of the country.

Norwegian is a Germanic language and belongs to the North Germanic group, which is closely related to Danish and Swedish. However, there are several variants of Norwegian, including Bokmål and Nynorsk, which are recognized as official written languages in Norway.

Bokmål, also known as "Book Norwegian", is the most commonly used written language in Norway. It is based on Danish and was developed in the 19th century as a way to standardize the Norwegian written language. Bokmål is mainly spoken and written in urban areas and in the south of Norway.

Nynorsk, or "New Norwegian", is another official written language in Norway and was developed in the 19th century in response to the dominance of Danish. It is based on the dialects and regional variants of Norwegian and is mainly used in rural areas and western Norway.

The Norwegian language is characterized by a relatively large number of dialects that vary from region to region. This reflects the geographical diversity of the country and means that Norwegians from different regions sometimes struggle to understand each other when speaking their own dialects.

An interesting feature of the Norwegian language is the use of umlauts, which are used to mark certain sounds. This can make pronunciation challenging for non-Norwegians, but it is an important part of spelling and pronunciation in Norway.

The Norwegian language has absorbed many influences throughout history, including Danish and Swedish. Nevertheless, it has retained its own identity and is a key to Norwegian culture and history.

Overall, the Norwegian language is an important aspect of Norwegian identity and a fascinating element of Norwegian culture. Their diversity and peculiarities make them an important feature of the country and help shape the national identity.

The importance of Norwegian in the modern world

The importance of Norwegian in the modern world is an interesting topic that looks at the role of this language in global contexts. Norwegian, as a North Germanic language, certainly does not have the worldwide distribution or economic importance as, for example, English or Spanish. Nevertheless, there are some important aspects that underline the importance of Norwegian in today's world.

First of all, Norwegian is the official language of Norway and therefore plays a central role in the country's daily life. It is used in schools, media, government affairs, and business. Norwegian is the primary form of communication between citizens and forms the basis of social and cultural life in Norway.

In addition, Norwegian is one of the official working languages of the Arctic Council Group, an international organization that represents the interests of Arctic states. This reflects Norway's importance as a country that plays an important role in the Arctic and contributes to the conservation of the Arctic and its resources.

Although Norwegian is not one of the most widely spoken languages in the world, there is still a strong Norwegian diaspora in various countries, including the United States, Canada, and Australia. These communities cultivate the Norwegian language and culture, which contributes to the worldwide spread of Norwegian.

Another aspect that underlines the importance of Norwegian in the modern world is the fact that Norway is a major player in international affairs. As a member of the United Nations, NATO and other international organizations, Norway plays an active role in international politics and diplomacy. The Norwegian language is used in these contexts as a means of communication and for diplomatic negotiations.

Finally, Norway is known as a popular tourist destination, and the Norwegian language may be of interest to travelers. While many Norwegians speak English, it can be useful for travelers to have some basic knowledge of Norwegian to better understand the culture and people.

Overall, Norwegian may not be one of the globally dominant languages, but it still has an important role in Norway and in international affairs. It is a key to Norwegian identity and contributes to Norway's connection with the world.

Norwegian dialects and regional differences

Norwegian dialects and regional differences are a fascinating feature of the Norwegian language and culture. Norway, with its diverse landscapes and geography, has given rise to a variety of dialects throughout history, often very different from each other.

The variety of Norwegian dialects is impressive. In fact, there are so many dialects in Norway that some linguists claim that there are as many Norwegian dialects as there are Norwegian valleys. This illustrates the strong connection between the dialects and the regional conditions of the country.

Norwegian dialects can be roughly divided into two main groups: Østnorsk (Eastern Norwegian) and Vestnorsk (Western Norwegian). Østnorsk is mainly spoken in the east and south of Norway and includes dialects such as Bokmål and Oslo dialects. Vestnorsk, on the other hand, is spoken in western Norway and includes dialects such as Nynorsk and the dialects in the fjords and mountains.

The dialects in Norway can differ significantly from each other in terms of pronunciation, vocabulary and grammar. As a result, Norwegians from different regions sometimes struggle to understand each other when speaking their own dialects. As a result, Norwegian, as a spoken language, is often closer to the dialects than the standardized written language.

The Norwegian dialects also reflect the cultural and historical differences between the regions of the country. People in the fjords often have their own dialect that is closely linked to their maritime way of life, while people in rural areas cultivate agricultural dialects. This diversity of dialects is an important part of Norwegian identity and culture.

More recently, the proliferation of mass media and the increasing mobility of the population has led to a certain convergence of dialects, especially in urban areas. Nevertheless, the diversity of Norwegian dialects remains an important cultural wealth of the country.

Overall, Norwegian dialects and regional differences are an exciting topic that reflects the diversity and cultural richness of Norway. They are a key to the country's identity and an interesting aspect of the Norwegian language and culture.

The Norwegian education and higher education system

The Norwegian education system is known for its high quality and focus on equal opportunities. Norway invests significantly in the education of its citizens and offers a wide range of educational opportunities at various levels.

Norway's education system is generally divided into three main levels: primary school (Barneskole), secondary school (Ungdomsskole) and secondary school (Videregående skole). Primary school usually lasts six years, followed by secondary school, which lasts three years. The secondary school is not only academically oriented, but also offers various vocational programs. After secondary school, students have the opportunity to apply to study at a college or university.

The Norwegian higher education system is characterised by its strong academic tradition and research orientation. Norway has a number of prestigious universities and colleges that offer a wide range of degree programs in various disciplines. Most colleges are state-funded, which means that tuition fees for Norwegian citizens are usually very low. This contributes to equal opportunities in the education system.

An interesting feature of the Norwegian education system is the emphasis on practical learning and vocational training. In addition to academic courses, there are a variety of vocational training opportunities that meet the needs of the job market in various industries. This opens up a wide range of career opportunities for graduates.

Another notable feature of the Norwegian education system is the emphasis on education for sustainable development and environmental issues. Norway attaches great importance to environmental awareness and sustainability and integrates these topics into the education system to prepare the next generation for the challenges of climate change and environmental degradation.

To sum up, the Norwegian education system is known for its quality, equal opportunities, and research orientation. It provides diverse educational opportunities to the country's citizens and promotes a wide range of skills and interests. The emphasis on practical experience, vocational training and environmental awareness makes it a contemporary and future-oriented education system.

The Norwegian Government and Political Structure

The Norwegian government and political structure are characterized by a long tradition of democracy and a strong welfare state. Norway is a parliamentary monarchy and has a stable political environment based on respect for the fundamental rights and freedoms of its citizens.

Norway's parliament, the Storting, is the country's highest legislative body. It consists of 169 members who are elected every four years. The Storting is responsible for legislation and budgetary control and plays a central role in Norwegian politics.

The monarch, currently King Harald V, has a mainly representative role in Norwegian politics. Actual political power lies with parliament and the elected government.

The Norwegian government is elected by parliament and consists of the prime minister and ministers. The Prime Minister is usually the leader of the largest party in the Storting and is appointed by the King. The government is responsible for the implementation of the laws and the administration of the country.

Norway has a multi-party democracy, and there are a variety of political parties represented in the Storting. The main parties are the Labour Party (Arbeiderpartiet), the Conservative Party (Høyre), the Progress Party (Fremskrittspartiet) and the Socialist Left Party (Sosialistisk Venstreparti). The political landscape can change from election to election as coalitions are formed to achieve a governing majority.

A significant feature of Norway's political structure is the principle of separation of powers, in which the executive, legislative, and judicial branches are separated from each other to ensure the rule of law and the independence of the judiciary.

Norway is also known for its strong emphasis on the welfare state. The country has a comprehensive social security system that provides health care, education, and social benefits to citizens. These social programs are widespread and contribute to a high standard of living in Norway.

Overall, the Norwegian government and political structure are characterized by stability, democracy and social responsibility. It has helped make Norway a prosperous and just country, internationally recognized for its political stability and welfare state.

Norway's social system and health care system

The Norwegian welfare system and health care system are fundamental pillars of the Norwegian welfare state and contribute significantly to the high standard of living and social justice in the country.

The healthcare system in Norway is based on the principle of universal health care, where all citizens have access to high-quality medical care, regardless of their income or social status. Health services are largely funded by the state and are tax-funded. This means that citizens do not have to bear high healthcare costs when they need medical treatment.

Healthcare in Norway is of high quality and the medical facilities are well equipped. There are a variety of hospitals, clinics, and doctors' offices throughout the country. Access to medical specialists and specialists is also guaranteed. The health system places great emphasis on prevention and health promotion, which helps to maintain the health of the population and prevent diseases.

In addition, the Norwegian welfare system offers a wide range of social benefits and support for citizens in different life situations. These include unemployment benefits, sick pay, pension benefits, child benefits, and support for people with disabilities. These benefits are designed to ensure the social security and well-being of citizens.

The Norwegian welfare system also promotes gender equality and work-life balance. Parents are entitled to generous parental leave and child benefit to facilitate childcare and support families.

In conclusion, Norway's welfare system and healthcare system are based on the principles of social justice and universal health care. They help to improve the quality of life of citizens and ensure social security in the country. These are important elements of the Norwegian welfare state, which is internationally regarded as exemplary.

Sustainability and environmental protection in Norway

Norway is known for its strong commitment to sustainability and environmental protection. The country has a long history of environmental awareness and has taken numerous measures to protect its natural resources and reduce environmental impact.

A crucial step towards environmental protection was Norway's accession to the Paris Agreement in 2016. The country has pledged to reduce its greenhouse gas emissions by 40% by 2030 and be carbon neutral by 2050. Norway is investing significant funds in renewable energy, especially hydropower, wind and solar energy, to reduce its dependence on fossil fuels.

Another important environmental protection project is the preservation of Norway's nature and biodiversity. Norway has stunning scenery ranging from fjords, forests, lakes to mountainous regions. These natural treasures are protected by extensive protected areas and national parks. These include places such as Jotunheimen National Park and Rondane National Park, which make an important contribution to the conservation of Norway's flora and fauna.

Norway is also a leader in fisheries and has strict regulations to protect fish stocks. The country is actively committed to sustainable fishing practices to ensure that marine resources are conserved in the long term.

Another impressive environmental protection project in Norway is the promotion of electromobility. Norway has one of the highest electric car densities in the world and offers numerous incentives for the purchase of electric vehicles, including tax benefits and free parking.

In addition, tourism plays an important role in Norway's environmental protection. The country specializes in promoting sustainable tourism and supporting eco-friendly practices to protect Norway's nature and culture.

Overall, Norway shows an impressive commitment to sustainability and environmental protection. The country is pursuing a comprehensive strategy to protect its natural resources, combat climate change, and minimize environmental impacts. This commitment to sustainability makes Norway a pioneer in this field and serves as a model for other countries worldwide.

The Norwegian economy and industry

Norway's economy and industry are characterized by a variety of characteristics that have made the country an economic success story. Norway, despite being a relatively small country, has a stable and prosperous economy that rests on various pillars.

One of the most important pillars of the Norwegian economy is the oil and gas industry. Norway is one of the largest exporters of crude oil and natural gas in the world and has become a major player in the global energy market. The discovery of large oil and gas deposits off the coast of Norway in the 1960s was a turning point for the country's economy. Revenues from energy exports have contributed to the formation of the so-called "oil fund", a sovereign wealth fund that accumulates significant assets for future generations and invests in various asset classes.

The maritime industry also plays an important role in Norway's economy. The country has a long coastline and a tradition in shipbuilding and shipping. Norwegian shipping companies and shipyards are internationally recognized and specialize in the construction of state-of-the-art vessels, from cargo ships to offshore platforms.

The fishing sector is another important industry in Norway. The country is one of the largest exporters of fish and seafood in the world. Norwegian salmon and cod are particularly in demand and can be found on menus in many countries.

The high-tech industry and the technology sector are also gaining importance. Norway's expertise in areas such as renewable energy, telecommunications, and software development has led to a growing number of start-ups and innovations.

The Norwegian economy is characterised by stable economic policies, a well-educated workforce and a strong social safety net. Despite its dependence on revenues from the oil and gas industry, Norway has successfully implemented diversification measures to make its economy more resilient.

To sum up, Norway's economy and industry are characterized by diversity, innovation, and smart resource management. This has helped to make the country a prosperous and economically stable country that enjoys international respect and recognition.

Norway's role in the international community

Norway plays an important role in the international community and has distinguished itself as a committed actor in many areas. As a member of various international organizations and alliances, the country has actively contributed to the promotion of peace, security and sustainable development.

One of the most important international organizations of which Norway is a member is the United Nations (UN). The country has repeatedly advocated multilateral cooperation and the strengthening of the role of the UN. Norway is a major donor of development aid and is committed to achieving the UN's Sustainable Development Goals by 2030.

Norway is also a member of NATO, the Nordic Councils and the Arctic Council. As a NATO member, Norway has contributed to the common defence and security in Europe. Norway plays a key role in the Arctic region, working to protect the fragile environment and promote dialogue between Arctic states.

The country is known for its active role in peace mediation and conflict resolution. Norway has been involved in peace negotiations and mediation processes in various parts of the world, including the Middle East, Sri Lanka and Colombia. These efforts have helped to end conflicts and promote peace.

Norway is also a pioneer in environmental protection and climate change. The country is committed to renewable energy, protecting the Arctic, and reducing greenhouse gas emissions. Norway is one of the countries with the highest shares of renewable energy in electricity generation and is investing in green technologies.

The Norwegian government is also involved in global health policy and supports international efforts to combat diseases such as HIV/AIDS, malaria and tuberculosis.

Norway has a good reputation in the international community as a country that is committed to human rights, democracy and social justice. The country has a long tradition of diplomacy and cooperation and will continue to play an important role in shaping the global agenda.

Epilogue

In the epilogue of this book about Norway, we would like to take a last look at this fascinating country. Norway, with its stunning nature, rich culture and remarkable history, undoubtedly has a lot to offer.

The geographical location of Norway, with its fjords, mountains and waterfalls, is of unique beauty. Norway's wildlife, from polar bears in the north to reindeer in the vastness of the country, is as diverse as it is impressive. Norwegian cuisine, characterized by fish and seafood, reflects the proximity to the sea and offers culinary delights for gourmets.

The history of Norway, from the Vikings to modern times, is marked by independence and cultural heritage. The country's cities, including Oslo, Bergen, Trondheim and Tromsø, are vibrant centres that harmoniously combine history and modernity.

The culture of Norway is characterized by its folklore, music and literature. The Norwegian language, characterized by regional dialects, is an important part of national identity. Norway has also made significant contributions to the world's art, music, and literature.

Norway's role in the international community is characterized by a commitment to peace, environmental protection and social justice. The country has established itself as a major player on the global stage and is committed to a sustainable future.

In this book, we have tried to give a comprehensive insight into Norway, showing its diversity and beauty, and highlighting the importance of this country in today's world. We hope that you enjoyed this trip through Norway and that you were inspired to explore this fascinating country for yourself.